FUN·TO·MAKE CRAFTS FOR EASTER

Boyds Mills Press

Editor
Tom Daning

Craft Contributors

Robin Adams
Patricia Barley
Katherine Corliss Bartow
Linda Bloomgren
Debra Boyles
Larry Dane Brimner
Jerry Brown
Barr Clay Bullock
Norma Jean Byrkett
KayLani Campbell
Marie Cecchini
Ann Clark
Bridget Hanley Cohen
Donna Collinsworth
Carol Conner
Evelyn Cook
Dee Francis

Sarah T. Frey
Mavis Grant
Mildred Grenier
Norah Grubmeyer
Joann Harper-McClellan
Edna Harrington
Joann M. Hart
Kathryn Heisenfelt
Texie Hering
Loretta Holz
Olive Howie
Helen Jeffries
Virginia Killough
Garnett Kooker
Virginia L. Kroll
Jean Kuhn
Judith L. LaDez

Twilla Lamm
Janet Rose Lehmberg
Ann Lewandowski
Richard Lewis
Ruth E. Libbey
Lee Lindeman
Agnes Maddy
Patricia A. McMillan
Ursula Michael
June Rose Mobly
Judith Morgan
Anita Page
Beatrice Bachrach Perri
James W. Perrin Jr.
Ellen Plausky
Karla P. Ray
Terry A. Ricioli

Kathy Ross
Laura Sassi
Barbara Smith
Cheryl Stees
Eve Stone
Debora Sullivan
Sister Mary Sylvia, V.S.C.
Marilyn Thomason
Mildred G. Turner
Sharon Dunn Umnik
Jan J. Van Pelt
Pamela Young Wolff
Agnes Choate Wonson
Connie Wright

Craft Builders
Verlie Hutchens
Jennifer Pereira

Copyright © 2005 by Boyds Mills Press
All rights reserved

Published by Boyds Mills Press, Inc.
A Highlights Company
815 Church Street
Honesdale, Pennsylvania 18431
Printed in China

Publisher Cataloging-in-Publication Data

Fun-to-make crafts for Easter / Boyds Mills Press.—1st ed.
[64] p.: col. photos. ; cm.
Includes index.
Summary: Includes step-by-step directions to make decorations, gifts, and
    greeting cards for Easter.
ISBN 1-59078-340-9
ISBN 1-59078-365-4 (pbk.)
1. Easter decorations — Juvenile literature. 2. Handicraft — Juvenile
    literature. I. Title.
745.594/1667 22   TT900.F86 2004

First edition, 2005
Book designed by Janet Moir McCaffrey
The text of this book is set in 11-point New Century Schoolbook.

Visit our Web site at www.boydsmillspress.com

10 9 8 7 6 5 4 3 2 1 hc
10 9 8 7 6 5 4 3 2 1 pb

*I*n these pages you will find more than 150 imaginative craft ideas for Easter and springtime. Gifts, games, toys, decorations, greeting cards—whatever you want to make, it's here. So put on your most stylish paint-splattered smock, roll up your sleeves, and create. Before you know it, Peter Cottontail will be hoppin' down the bunny trail!

Safety First

Although most crafts in this book are designed for you to make yourself, remember to ask for an adult's help when handling sharp instruments or using the stove.

Follow the Directions— But Add Your Own Flair

To build each craft, follow the steps listed. The directions and the pictures are helpful guides, but they are no substitute for your own imagination. You might figure out a different way to make a bunny's ears or to decorate your Easter eggs. Or you might be inspired to make up your own crafts.

Neatness Counts

Before you get crafty, be smart and cover your work area. Old newspapers, brown paper bags, old sheets, or a plastic drop cloth will work. Protect your clothes with an apron, a smock, or a big old shirt. And remember to clean up after you are finished.

Stock Your Craft Workshop

We've included a list of materials to make each craft. Recyclable items such as cardboard tubes, plastic milk bottles, and cereal boxes are needed for many of them. Before you start, check out the items in the materials list for the crafts you plan to make. Ask your parents, friends, and relatives to start saving these things for you, so you will always have a supply on hand. If you don't have the exact item listed, something else may work just as well. Make sure you clean and dry the recyclables before using them. Also, good crafters usually keep some supplies handy—such as scissors, crayons, markers, craft glue, tape, pens, pencils, paint, a hole punch, and a stapler. Because these are used so frequently, we don't include them in the list of materials.

Have Fun!

Eggs, Eggs, and More Eggs . . .

Making a Hard-Boiled Egg

stove ● saucepan ● water ● whole raw egg

1. Have an adult help you use the stove. Fill a saucepan halfway with cool water. Place the egg in the pan and bring the water to a slow boil, using low heat.
2. Cook the egg for seven minutes from the boiling point. Remove the pan from the heat and let the egg cool.

Blowing Out the Inside of an Egg

large sewing needle ● whole raw egg ● large bowl ● water

1. Stick a large sewing needle into the pointed end of a raw egg, making sure to poke through the membrane under the shell. Then stick the needle through the other end, making a larger hole than the first.
2. Over a large bowl, blow through the small hole, allowing the inside of the egg to flow into the bowl. Carefully rinse the shell in cold water.

Dyeing Eggs with Food Coloring

coffee mug or small bowl ● measuring spoons ● white vinegar ● hot water ● food coloring ● blown or hard-boiled eggs ● spoon

1. In a coffee mug or small bowl, add 1 teaspoon of white vinegar to 1 cup of hot water from the kitchen tap. Place several drops of food coloring into the hot water.
2. Place an egg in the mixture. Hold the egg down gently with a spoon.
3. When the egg reaches the color you want, remove it and let it dry on a paper towel.

Grass Head

eggshell ● potting soil ● grass seed ● water ● bottle cap

1. Wash a large piece of eggshell, and set it aside to dry.
2. Paint a face on the shell with markers.
3. To make "hair," fill the shell with potting soil to within ¼ inch of the top. Scatter grass seed on it. Cover the seeds with a thin layer of soil. Drip water onto the soil.
4. Place the egghead on a small upside-down bottle cap. Put it in a window that gets morning sun. In several days, "hair" will sprout.

Color Chart

To make:	Combine:
LIME GREEN	1 drop green + 3 drops yellow
ORANGE	2 drops red + 3 drops yellow
TURQUOISE	1 drop green + 4 drops blue
VIOLET	2 drops red + 2 drops blue

Experiment on your own to find other colors.

Ham and Egg

construction paper ● blown egg ● chenille stick ● cardboard egg carton

1. To make a piglet, cut and glue construction-paper features on a blown egg. Glue on a small piece of chenille stick for the tail.
2. Cut a cup section from a cardboard egg carton, and paint it for the pig's feet. Glue the egg to the feet.

Flower Power Eggs

● colorful napkin ● blown egg ● water

1. Cut or tear a colorful napkin into small pieces. Carefully hold a piece of the napkin on the shell of a blown-out egg.
2. Dip a finger into some watered-down glue and "paint" over the napkin piece with it. The glue will soak through, and the napkin will stick to the egg. Cover about half of the egg and allow it to dry. Then cover the other half. Let dry.

Tie-Dye Eggs

old T-shirt or sheet ● hard-boiled eggs ● egg-dyeing mixture (page 4) ● egg carton ● shortening ● paper towel

1. With an adult's help and permission, tear narrow strips from an old clean T-shirt or sheet.
2. Cover your work area with a thick layer of newspaper.
3. Twist and wrap the strips of cloth around a hard-boiled egg several times, and knot them in place. Continue until the egg is completely covered.
4. Make up the egg-dyeing mixture on page 4. Place each wrapped egg into the mixture. Let the egg sit in the dye for about twenty minutes.
5. Remove the egg with a spoon. Then take off the cloth strips. Set the egg in an egg carton until dry. Polish the egg with a bit of shortening on a paper towel.
6. For a variation, place stickers on the egg before wrapping it. Remove the stickers after taking off the cloth strips. The egg will not be colored wherever the stickers were placed.

Shelly

hard-boiled egg ● permanent markers ● yarn

1. Sketch features on a hard-boiled egg. Color them with permanent markers.
2. Glue on yarn for hair.

Spring-Flower Mobile

large box ● construction paper ● yarn
● four small boxes

1. Cover a large box with glue and construction paper. Poke two holes, one opposite the other, in the middle of the narrow sides of the box. Glue the ends of a piece of yarn into each hole to form a hanger. Glue a strip of paper around the top of the box, covering the yarn on each side, to help hold the hanger in place.
2. Cover four small boxes with glue and paper. Create paper flowers and glue them to the boxes. With a pencil, poke a hole in the top of each box and glue a piece of yarn into each hole.
3. Poke four holes in the bottom of the large box. Insert the yarn ends from the four small boxes and glue them in place. Let dry.

Easter Pop-up Card

1¼" →I

poster board

1. Fold two pieces of poster board in half horizontally. Draw an egg shape on the outside of one piece. Slip the second piece inside the first, and holding them steady, cut both pieces into the egg shape.
2. Decorate the first shape as an Easter egg.
3. On the other egg shape, cut two slits, each 2½ inches long and about 1¼ inches apart, on the folded edge as shown. Bend the flap back and forth. Then push the flap through the card to make the pop-up.
4. From a piece of yellow poster board, draw and cut out a chick to fit inside the card.
5. Glue the two cards together, being sure not to glue the pop-up flap. Add an Easter greeting inside the card. Glue the chick to the pop-up flap.

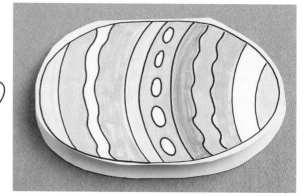

Goodie Basket

half-gallon milk carton ● construction paper

1. To make the basket, cut a half-gallon milk carton in half.
2. For the handle, cut a 1-inch-wide section from the leftover part of the milk carton. Cut away one side of this section.
3. Cover the basket and handle with construction paper. Glue the handle to the basket. Decorate with cut-paper designs.

Handy Lamb Puppet

paper ● small brown paper bag

1. Draw and cut the lamb's head and ears from paper. Add eyes, a nose, and a mouth.
2. To make the lamb's curls, cut strips of paper and curl them by wrapping them around a pencil. Glue them between the lamb's ears. Glue the head to the bottom of the paper bag.
3. Cut the body from paper and glue it to the front of the bag. Add paper feet.

Snow Bunny

4-inch and 3-inch plastic-foam balls ● craft sticks ● pompoms ● yarn ● chenille sticks ● felt ● buttons

1. Shave the bottom of a 4-inch plastic-foam ball flat so that it will stand. Push a craft stick into the top of it until about 1½ inches stick out.
2. Push the 3-inch foam ball onto the craft stick for the head. Glue on pompoms for the eyes and nose, and add yarn for the mouth. Make arms with chenille sticks and insert them into the body.
3. Cut out two ear shapes from white felt. Glue them to the top half of both sides of a craft stick. Do the same to make the other ear. Add pink felt for inner ears. Push the ends of the craft sticks into the bunny's head.
4. Cut a strip of felt for the scarf. Cut the ends to make fringe. Wrap the scarf around the bunny's neck and glue in place. Add buttons for trim.

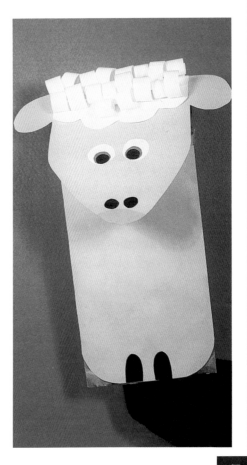

Bunny Pin or Necklace

wooden ice-cream spoon ● heavy white paper ● cotton ● ribbon ● safety pin

1. Paint a wooden ice-cream spoon white and let dry. Draw and cut two ear shapes and four paw shapes from heavy white paper. Add details.
2. Add facial features to the large end of the spoon. Glue the ends of the ears and paws to the back of the spoon. Glue a small piece of cotton to the bottom of the spoon for a fluffy tail. If you like, you can glue a small ribbon scrap to the bunny's head for a bow.
3. To make a necklace, glue the ends of a piece of ribbon to the back of the bunny's head. Make the loop large enough to fit over your head. To make a pin, glue a safety pin to the back of the spoon.

Spring-Fling Bag

fabric ● tape or pins ● embroidery floss ● embroidery needle ● felt ● shoelace

1. Cut a piece of fabric about 22 inches long and 14 inches wide. Fold a ¾-inch hem underneath the right side of the fabric at each short end. Use pieces of tape or pins to hold in place. Sew together with embroidery floss using straight stitches, as shown.
2. Cut flowers, stems, and leaves from felt. Sew them to the top half of the right side of the fabric. Leave a 2-inch border around the edges. Turn the flower side over. Fold a ¾-inch hem toward the wrong side of the fabric on each long side and hold with tape or pins.
3. With the right side out, fold the fabric in half. Stitch the sides together. Remove the tape or pins.
4. To make the handle, cut a long shoelace in half. Sew one piece to each side of the bag.

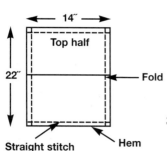

Hand Lilies

construction paper

1. Trace around your hand on construction paper. Cut out the shape.
2. Cut a stamen from yellow paper. Place it on the paper hand.
3. Fold over the edges of the hand at the bottom. Glue or staple them in place, with the stamen in the middle. Curl the petals around a pencil.
4. Cut out paper stems and leaves. Arrange everything on a piece of paper, and glue in place.

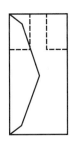

Easter Egg Hunt

cardboard ● felt

1. Cut a piece of cardboard to measure 18 inches by 12 inches. Spread glue on one side, and cover it with a piece of felt. Trim the edges with scissors, or tape them to the back.
2. To make the picture, cut pieces of felt in the shape of a rabbit, basket, chick, tree, clouds, stone wall—or other items—and place them on the felt board.
3. Cut out small felt eggs. Hide them behind the felt objects in your picture.
4. Let your friends take turns searching for the eggs. Change the picture over and over.

Basket in an Envelope

long white envelope ● plastic grass

1. Moisten the flap of a long white envelope and seal it shut. Cut out two sections of the envelope, as shown.

2. Decorate the basket. Fill it with plastic grass.

Bunny Topper

cotton balls ● construction paper ● pencil ● small paper cup ● chenille stick ● plastic grass ● beads

1. Glue two cotton balls together. Cut features and ears from construction paper. Glue them to the top cotton ball. Let dry.
2. Tape the bottom cotton ball to the top of a pencil.
3. To make the basket, poke the pencil point down through the bottom of a small paper cup and slide the cup up the pencil.
4. Add a handle by punching a hole on opposite sides of the cup, just below the rim. Put the ends of a 6-inch piece of chenille stick through the holes, and wrap them up and around the rim.
5. Glue plastic grass inside the basket (but don't glue it to the pencil). Glue beads inside the basket to look like jelly beans.
6. Hold the cup with one hand, and move the pencil up and down with the other to make the rabbit appear or disappear.

Caterpillar to Cocoon to Butterfly

fallen tree branch ● chenille sticks ● tissue paper ● waxed paper

1. Find a small twiggy branch. For the caterpillar, fold a green chenille stick in half. Slip it over a twig and twist it. Wrap the other end around the twig.
2. For the cocoon, wrap two tan chenille sticks to a second twig to create a cocoonlike bulge.
3. Cut a butterfly shape out of three layers of tissue paper. Place the shapes on waxed paper. Glue them together by coating them with a thin layer of watered-down glue. Cut shapes from brightly colored tissue paper folded for double thickness. Place the cutouts on the butterfly. Gently coat the butterfly with watered-down glue.
4. When dry, carefully peel it off the waxed paper. Then fold a brown chenille stick in half. Slip it over the butterfly between the wings. Twist both ends to make antennae and a tail.
5. Secure the butterfly to a branch by bending the tail and antennae around a twig. Place in a tall slender vase.

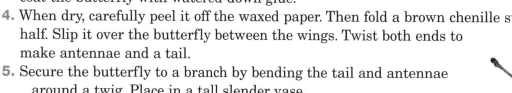

Yarn Card

poster board ● yarn

1. Fold a piece of poster board in half to make a card.
2. Draw and cut out an egg shape from another piece of poster board. Spread several lines of white glue on the egg shape, dividing it into sections. Press black yarn into the glue.
3. Fill the sections with glue, and press pieces of yarn into the glue, starting at the outline of each section and moving toward the middle.
4. Glue the egg to the front of the card. Add a message.

Bunny Mask

platter ● poster board ● construction paper ● yarn

1. Place a platter on a piece of poster board, and trace around the edge. Cut out the shape. Cut a slit from both sides to the center, as shown. On one side of the mask, pull the edge of the slit over the top of the other edge. Glue the edges in place. Do the same for the other side, making a small cone in the center of the mask.
2. From construction paper, cut two large white circles and two smaller dark circles for eyes and two triangle shapes for eyebrows. Glue them in place.
3. Cut holes to see through in the center of each paper eye. Add ears, whiskers, and a mouth made from paper.
4. Poke a hole in each side of the mask and add yarn ties.

Slits

Place-Card Chick

plastic egg ● chenille stick ● construction paper

1. Glue the top and bottom of a plastic egg together, as shown. Wrap a piece of a chenille stick around the center for support.
2. Cut a chick from construction paper. Add features with paper, and glue the chick inside the cup.
3. Print a guest's name on a piece of paper, and glue it to the front of the cup.

Wrapping-Paper Card

construction paper ● gift wrap

1. On a piece of folded construction paper, cut out an egg shape, with the left side on the fold.
2. Cut out flower shapes from bits of gift wrap, and glue them to the front of the egg. Cut a vase and leaves from construction paper, and glue them in place. Draw stems.
3. Write an Easter message inside the card.

Easter Critter Candy Jar

ribbon ● baby-food jar ● plastic grass ● cotton balls ● felt ● small pompom ● jelly beans

1. Glue a piece of ribbon around the lid of a baby-food jar and tie it into a bow. Glue plastic grass to the lid.
2. Glue two small cotton balls together. To make a bird, add felt eyes and a beak, and feathers for wings. For a rabbit, glue on a pompom tail and felt features. Glue the bird or rabbit to the lid and let dry.
3. Fill the jar with jelly beans.

Bunny Hop

white paper ● construction paper ● colored pens

1. Cut a piece of white paper 6 inches by 12 inches. Fold in half three times to 6 inches by 3 inches.
2. Draw and cut out half a bunny shape on the fold, but don't cut the ends of the arms.
3. Cut dresses, hair bows, slacks, suspenders, and bow ties from paper. Glue them to the bunnies. Add features with colored pens.

Butterfly Hand Puppet

felt ● chenille sticks ● needle ● thread ● old sock

1. Cut a butterfly shape out of felt.
2. Cut pieces of felt to decorate the butterfly. Cut through two pieces of felt at the same time for each design so that your butterfly's wings will look the same. Glue the cut pieces onto the felt.
3. Twist together two chenille sticks to make a body and antennae. Sew the sticks onto the butterfly, tucking the end of the body underneath the felt.
4. Cut off the cuff from an old sock. Turn the cuff inside out and sew the cut end shut. Turn the cuff right side out.
5. Sew the back of the butterfly to the cuff. Put your hand in the cuff, and make your butterfly fly by gently moving your hand up and down.

Sock Hopper

old tube sock ● cardboard ● plastic-foam balls ● string ● ribbon

1. Measure 8 inches up from the toe of an old tube sock. Cut off the extra material at the top. Turn the sock wrong side out.
2. Cut two pieces of cardboard 4 inches long and 1 inch wide. Round the ends. Glue one over the other. Put them inside the sock across the toe area.
3. For the body, put a 3-inch plastic-foam ball into the sock on top of the feet. For the tail, put a 1-inch plastic-foam ball into the sock at the back of the larger ball. Use string to gather the sock around the tail and above the feet.
4. Use smaller plastic-foam balls to make paws at the sides of the large plastic-foam ball. Gather the sock around each paw and tie with string.
5. Put a 2½-inch plastic-foam ball in the sock for the head. Pull the top of the sock to the back of the head and tie with string.
6. To make ears, cut the top of the sock in two and tie each section at the top.
7. Decorate with paper, string, ribbon, and marker.

13

Pompom Chick

yarn ● cardboard ● construction paper ● chenille stick ● wiggle eyes

1. Make two pompoms. For each, wrap yarn around your palm about fifty times. Slip the pompom off your hand and tie it tightly around the middle. Snip the loops and fluff.
2. Cut a chick shape from cardboard. Trace and cut out the chick twice on construction paper.
3. On the cardboard chick, make a vertical slit at the crook of the neck. Fold an orange chenille stick in half. Bend the ends to look like feet. Insert the legs into the slit, tugging gently to secure.
4. Glue the paper chicks to the sides of the cardboard chick, covering the legs. Then apply glue to both sides of the chick, and press the pompoms in place. Set under a heavy book to dry.
5. Color the beak and add wiggle eyes. Bend the legs to make it stand.

Raggedy Rabbit

washcloth ● safety pin ● heavy thread ● needle ● cotton ● felt

1. Roll in two sides of a washcloth tightly to the center. Pin in the middle with a safety pin.
2. To make the ears, hold the rolled sides down and push the cloth down between the rolls halfway to the pin. Tie each ear at the base with heavy thread.
3. Tie the cloth in the middle to form the head, and remove the pin. Open out the head, stuff with cotton, and sew shut.
4. For the legs, open the rolled ends slightly, tuck a thin layer of cotton up into each side, and roll tightly again. With the rolled side down, push up the cloth between the rolls to the "tummy" and sew it to the legs.
5. Open the body and stuff with cotton. Sew up the back. Add features to the rabbit's face with felt. Use thread for the whiskers. Add a felt bow under his chin.
6. Cut a coat from felt and sew up the sides. Stuff cotton-ball hands in the sleeves, and sew in place. Sew on a cotton ball for the tail. Add a felt scarf.

Sew along the dotted line.

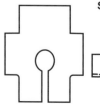

Peek-a-boo Duck Card

construction paper

1. Fold a piece of construction paper in half. Cut out an egg, keeping the top on the fold.
2. Open the egg and cut a jagged window out of the front. Close the egg and write "Hi!" under the window. Punch out paper dots and glue them around the window.
3. Cut out a circle of paper just large enough to fill the window. Glue on a paper beak and eyes, and glue the duck's head inside the card.
4. Write "Happy Easter" on a piece of paper. Glue it to the front of the duck. Add paper wings and feet.

Mama Mutton and Lil' Lamb

cardboard ● cotton balls ● felt ● ribbon

1. For each sheep, cut two matching shapes from cardboard. Glue the shapes together except for the feet.
2. Glue cotton balls on both sides of the sheep. From felt, cut ears, eyes, cheeks, a nose, a mouth, and feet. Glue them on the sheep. Add a ribbon to each sheep.
3. Bend the feet out until the sheep can stand.

Bunny-Hop Game

sandpaper ● plastic measuring cup ● yarn ● table-tennis ball ● cotton ● felt ● wiggle eyes ● construction paper

1. Glue sandpaper around a plastic measuring cup from a box of powdered detergent.
2. Cut a 15-inch-long piece of yarn. Glue one end inside the cup, opposite the handle. Glue the other end to a table-tennis ball.
3. To make a bunny, glue cotton over the yarn on the ball. Create a face on the ball with markers, felt, and wiggle eyes. Glue on cut-paper ears.
4. Cut fringe in a strip of green paper. Glue it around the cup.

Easter-Egg Weave

construction paper

1. On a 9-by-12-inch sheet of construction paper, draw the lines as shown in the diagram to begin the basket. Cut along the lines with scissors.

Cut slits as shown.

Egg with tab

Cut lines.

2. Cut strips measuring 4½ inches by ½ inch from two colors of paper. Weave these in and out of the slits to form a basket. Glue the ends in place.

3. Cut an 11-inch strip of paper for the handle. Bend it in half and glue it to the basket.
4. Draw and cut out paper eggs, each with a tab as shown. Cut slits above the basket and slip the eggs in them. Turn over the paper, and glue the tabs in place.
5. Bend the handle and eggs forward so they stand away from the background.

Jumbo Easter Chick

large juice can ● felt ● cardboard ● ribbon

1. Cover the sides and top of a large juice can with felt. Cut out two black eyes and an orange beak from felt and glue them to the front of the can.
2. Cut out two wing shapes from cardboard and glue felt on both sides. Glue a wing to each side of the can.
3. Trace the bottom of the can onto cardboard. Draw two feet extending from the circle. Cut out the shape as one piece. Trace the shape onto felt and cut it out. Glue the cardboard and felt feet together, then glue the feet to the bottom of the can. Glue on a bow tie made from ribbon.

Bunny-and-Pals Mobile

two plastic drinking straws ● dental floss ● foam paper

1. Place two plastic drinking straws together to form an X. Wrap dental floss around the center, adding glue.
2. Cut four eggs, four chicks, and a rabbit from foam paper. Decorate them. Punch a hole in the top of each shape.
3. Using short pieces of dental floss, tie the eggs to the ends of the straws. Using longer pieces of floss, tie the chicks halfway between the ends and the center. Using an even longer piece of floss, tie the rabbit to the center of the X.
4. Fold two long threads in half and tie them together, making a loop at the fold. Tie the four ends to the ends of the straws.

Craft-Stick Basket

poster board ● craft sticks ● cardboard ● plastic grass

1. Cut matching rectangles from poster board.
2. Cut tabs ¼ inch long and the width of a craft stick apart into the short ends of each rectangle. Fold back every other tab.
3. To make the other two sides of the basket, use a dot of glue to attach one end of a craft stick to each folded tab on one rectangle. Glue the other end of each stick to the folded tabs on the other rectangle.
4. Cut a piece of cardboard to fit the bottom of the basket. Tape it in place.
5. Cut out and glue on a poster-board handle. Line the bottom of the basket with plastic grass.

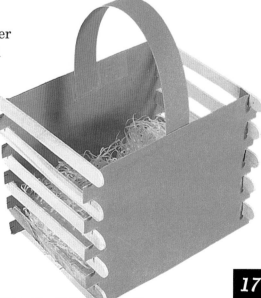

Egg Holder

cardboard egg carton ● construction paper

1. To make a special cup for Easter eggs, cut two cup sections from a cardboard egg carton.
2. Trim one evenly for the base. Trim the other to look like flower petals. Glue the two cups with their bottoms together.
3. Cover the cups with poster paint. When dry, decorate with paper-punch dots.

Egg-Tac-Toe

poster board ● cardboard ●
magnetic strips ● craft sticks

1. Draw ten egg shapes on poster board. (Make one egg template to trace the shapes so that they are all the same size.) Color five eggs in the same design and five eggs in another.
2. Glue the poster board onto cardboard. Place under a heavy book and let dry completely. Cut out the eggs, and glue magnetic strips to the back of each egg.
3. Glue the craft sticks together to make a tic-tac-toe grid. Paint the grid and let dry. Add magnetic strips to the back of the overlapped sticks.
4. Grab a friend and play Egg-Tac-Toe on a metal surface, such as your refrigerator or a cookie sheet.

Cone Bunny

construction paper ● cotton ball

1. Cut a half circle from construction paper. Roll the half circle into a cone shape and tape the ends together. Use a marker to add facial features.
2. Draw and cut four paw shapes from construction paper. Add details to the paws with black marker. Tape the ends of two of the paws to the inside of the bottom of the cone. Fold these up to lie flat for the rabbit's feet. Tape the ends of the other two paws to the sides of the cone, and fold the paws up. Add a cotton-ball tail.
3. To make the ears, cut a rectangle from construction paper. Fold the rectangle in half. Start from the folded end and cut a rabbit-ear shape. Cut a half circle out of the folded end, creating two ear shapes when the paper is unfolded.
4. Color the inside of each ear with marker and slide the hole over the cone. If you like, you can glue the ears in place near the point.

Colorful Chick Card

white paper ● construction paper

1. On a piece of folded white paper, draw a chick with its back on the fold. Cut it out. Color the chick's front yellow, its eye black, and its beak orange.
2. Fold a piece of construction paper for a card. Glue the chick to the front.
3. Cut out and glue on tail feathers. Cut one wing on a fold of yellow paper, and glue it to the chick. Add legs and feet with a marker.
4. Outline the edge of the inside of the chick with yellow marker. Write "Easter Greetings" on the inside of the chick. Write a message inside the card.

Lil' Easter Basket

plastic food container ● two chenille sticks ● felt ● ribbon ● plastic grass

1. Punch a hole on both sides of a plastic food container near the top with a hole punch.
2. Wrap two chenille sticks around each other, insert each end into a hole, and twist the ends together for the handle.
3. Glue pieces of felt to the outside of the container.
4. Decorate the handle with ribbon and a bow. Fill the basket with plastic grass and treats.

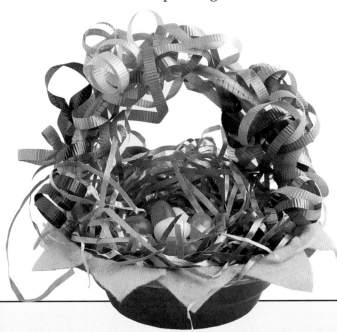

"Attractive" Rabbit

plastic-foam egg carton ● heavy paper ● felt ● broom straw ● magnetic strip

1. Cut two egg cups from a plastic-foam egg carton.
2. To make the rabbit shape, draw circles that are larger than an egg cup on heavy paper. Add ears and feet. Cut out the paper rabbit pattern.
3. Place the pattern on a piece of felt, and trace around it with a pencil. Cut out the felt rabbit.
4. Glue the two egg cups on the rabbit. Add features from felt and whiskers from broom straw. Glue a magnetic strip to the back.
5. Place your rabbit on the refrigerator door.

Curled-Paper Sheep Card

construction paper ● wiggle eye ● white paper

1. Fold a piece of colored construction paper in half. Lightly draw an oval on the front for your sheep's body.
2. Cut a head and four legs from black construction paper. Glue them to the body. Add a small wiggle eye.
3. For the wool, cut long narrow strips from white paper. Curl each strip tightly around a pencil, then gently release so the curl loosens slightly. Dab the outer end with glue and press the curl closed.
4. Spread glue onto your oval. Place each curl firmly into the glue until the oval is filled.
5. When dry, open your card and write an Easter message.

Hill of Beans

plastic-foam cup ● old CD ●
construction paper ● jelly beans

1. Paint the outside of a plastic-foam cup and let dry. Turn it upside down and glue it to the shiny side of an old CD.
2. Draw and cut out a small bunny from construction paper. Fold a tab at the bottom of the bunny, and glue it to the top of the cup.
3. Glue jelly beans to the outside of the cup.

Double Chick

cardboard ● cardboard tube

1. Cut two identical chicks from cardboard. Cover them with poster paint and let dry. Add eyes, beaks, and wings cut from painted cardboard.
2. Cut a 1-inch section from a cardboard tube. Paint it, let dry, then glue it between the chicks.

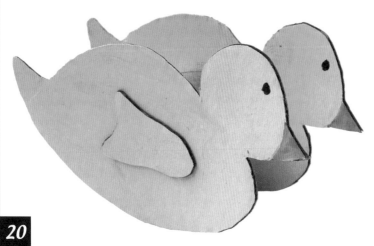

Stained-Glass Cross

poster board ● old newspaper ● white tissue paper ●
plastic spray bottle ● water ● food coloring ● string

1. Draw and cut out a cross from a piece of poster board. Cut out small shapes using scissors and a hole punch.
2. Place sheets of old newspaper on your work surface. Lay white tissue, larger than the cross, on top of the newspaper.
3. Fill a spray bottle with water and moisten the tissue paper with a fine mist, making it damp, not wet. Sprinkle drops of food coloring on the tissue paper and let dry.
4. Put a thin layer of glue on one side of the cross and lay it on the tissue paper. Trim the edges. Punch a hole at the top and attach a string hanger.
5. Hang the cross in a window.

String Basket

string ● plastic bag ● balloon ● plastic cup ● glitter

1. Put a ball of string in a plastic bag. Pour in about ½ cup of glue, colored with food coloring, if you like. Seal the bag closed. Knead the bag with your hand to cover the string with glue.
2. Blow up a medium-sized balloon. Tie it closed.
3. Open the bag just enough to pull out the end of the string. Wrap the balloon with the string, pulling out more from the bag as you need it. Wrap it in different directions and cross the string over itself. When you've used all the string (or you're satisfied with how much you've wrapped the balloon), tuck the end under a string wrap, using extra glue if needed to hold it in place.
4. Set the string-covered balloon on top of a plastic cup. Sprinkle it with glitter. Let it dry overnight. When dry, pop the balloon. Throw away the balloon pieces.
5. Cut away the top sides of the shape to make a basket.

Foam Easter Basket

plastic-foam egg cartons ● paper ● chenille stick

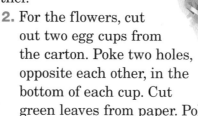

1. For the base of the basket, cut two end sections from the lid of a plastic-foam egg carton. Overlap the sections and glue them together.

2. For the flowers, cut out two egg cups from the carton. Poke two holes, opposite each other, in the bottom of each cup. Cut green leaves from paper. Poke a hole through the middle of each leaf.

3. For the handle, thread the flowers and leaves onto a long chenille stick. Poke holes in opposite sides of the basket, thread chenille-stick ends through, and twist into place.

Bubble-Gum Bunny Magnet

pink chenille sticks ● pink bubble-gum container ● pompoms ● wiggle eyes ● magnetic strip

1. Fold two pink chenille sticks into ear shapes. Insert the ends into the top of a bubble-gum container and squeeze shut, using tape to hold the container closed.

2. Glue on pompoms for the nose and cheeks. Glue on wiggle eyes. Let dry.

3. Glue a magnetic strip to the back. Let dry.

Flowery Springtime Card

construction paper ● old greeting cards or catalogs

1. For your card, fold a piece of paper in half.

2. Cut out pictures of flower blossoms from old greeting cards or catalogs.

3. Glue the blossoms onto the front of the card. Draw stems, leaves, a border, and other decorations.

4. Write a message inside.

Ring-Toss Rabbit

cardboard ● cardboard tube ● rubber bands ● poster board

1. Cut a head, front paws, and back paws for the rabbit from a piece of cardboard. Paint them white and let dry. Add details with paint and markers.
2. For the body, paint a cardboard tube white and let dry. Cut two vertical slits almost in the middle of the tube. Insert the front paws through the slits.
3. Glue the head and the back paws to the body. Hold in place with rubber bands until dry. Glue the rabbit to a square cardboard base.
4. Cut strips of poster board, and tape them together to form rings. Make up a point system for the game. For example, a ring on an ear might be worth 10 points and one on a paw, 15 points.

Foam-Egg Mobile

plastic-foam egg carton ● colored tissue paper ● string ● wide plastic container ● yarn

1. Cut cups from a plastic-foam egg carton. For each egg, glue two cups together.
2. Cut designs from colored tissue paper and glue them to the eggs.
3. Attach a string to each egg for a hanger. Tie all the eggs to a ring cut from a wide plastic container.
4. Punch four evenly spaced holes in the ring, and tie a length of yarn into each hole. Tie the pieces of yarn together at the top to hang the mobile.

Rascally Rabbit

cardboard tube ●
heavy white paper ●
cotton ball ● construction paper

1. Paint a cardboard tube with poster paint and let dry. Cut four legs, two ears, and a circle from heavy white paper. Paint them and let dry.
2. Place the tube end on the circle and draw around the outside. Cut out the circle. This will be the head.
3. Glue the head, with the ears in between, at one end of the tube. Glue the legs on each side of the tube. Add a cotton-ball tail.
4. Cut out paper features, and glue them to the head.

Nuts About Eggs

pecans in shells ● plastic bottle cap ● pliers ● large paper clip

1. Ask an adult to help you place pecans in boiling water. Turn off the water and let stand for a few hours. (This removes the shiny surface from the nuts so the paint will stick to them.)
2. Paint the nuts however you like. Create details with a small paintbrush, a cotton swab, a toothpick, or whatever you can think of.
3. Use a plastic bottle cap as a stand for drying the nuts in between coats.
4. With the help of an adult, use pliers to reshape a large paper clip into a spiral display stand for the nut "eggs."

24

Tulip Ring

sixteen craft sticks ●
construction paper ●
tissue paper

1. Paint sixteen craft sticks
   and let them dry.
2. Glue two of the sticks
   together at the center so
   they form an X. Continue
   to form X's with the
   remaining sticks.
3. Make the wreath by
   arranging the X's in a
   circle and gluing them
   together, end to end.
4. Cut and glue
   construction-paper tulips
   and leaves. Make a bow
   from tissue paper, and
   glue it to the wreath.

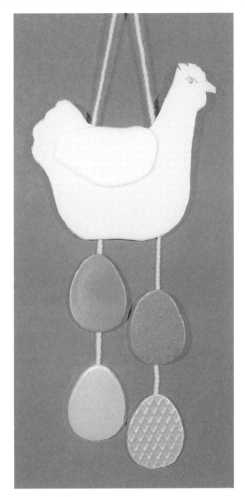

Chick Mobile

plastic-foam trays ● yarn

1. Cut out the shapes of a chicken,
   its wing, and eggs from plastic-
   foam trays of different colors.
2. Draw an eye on the chicken, and
   glue on its wing. Attach the eggs
   to the chicken by taping yarn to
   the back of them.
3. Hang the mobile from a piece of
   yarn taped to the back of
   the chicken.

Bunny Bonnet

poster board ● construction paper ●
paper doily ● foam paper

1. Cut a rabbit face from poster board. Add
   pink ears from construction paper.
2. Glue a small paper doily over the rabbit's
   face. Add paper eyes, nose, mouth, and
   whiskers.
3. Cut a long strip of foam paper, and glue
   the rabbit to the center of the strip.
   Staple the ends of the strip together
   so that it fits around your head.

Cuddly Bunny Pillow

two handkerchiefs ● large-eye needle ● yarn ● ribbon ● cotton balls or batting ● felt

1. Place one large handkerchief on top of another. Thread a large-eye needle with yarn. Sew the handkerchiefs together on three sides. Knot each yarn end.
2. To form ears, tie each sewn corner with ribbon.
3. Use cotton balls or batting to stuff the head section. Tightly tie the opening closed with yarn. Add a ribbon bow over the yarn.
4. Cut out felt shapes for the eyes, nose, and inside of the ears. Glue them to the head. Use markers to add a mouth and eyelashes.

Giant Egg Decoration

plastic ham container ● cardboard ● felt

1. Wash and dry a plastic ham container. Ask an adult to help you, as the edges of the container may be sharp.
2. Cut out a piece of cardboard to cover the front of the container. Glue it in place.
3. Cover the entire container with felt. Decorate it to look like an Easter egg.

Sowing the Seeds of Love

construction paper ● package of flower seeds

1. For the card, fold a piece of construction paper in half. Fold up a strip about 2 inches from the bottom to make a pocket inside.
2. Decorate the front of the card with markers.
3. Place a package of flower seeds in the pocket inside the card and write a message.

Peter Cotton-Ball Pin

cardboard ● cotton ball ● wiggle eyes ● construction paper ● safety pin

1. Cut a small circle from a piece of cardboard. Glue a cotton ball on top.
2. To make the rabbit's face, glue on two wiggle eyes and ears and whiskers made from construction paper.
3. Glue a small safety pin to the back of the cardboard. Attach the rabbit to your shirt.

Cool Easter Fan

five craft sticks ● construction paper ● ribbon

1. Arrange five craft sticks in a fan shape. Glue the sticks together at the bottom where they meet and let dry.
2. Lay the sticks on a piece of construction paper, and trace around the fan shape. Cut out the fan shape and decorate it with cut paper.
3. Glue the paper fan on the craft sticks. Make a ribbon bow, and glue it to the bottom of the fan.

Circle Chick

construction paper

1. Cut a circle from yellow construction paper and six triangles from orange paper. Cut a rectangle from orange paper.
2. Glue two triangles to the left side of the circle for the beak and one triangle to the right side of the circle for the tail. Turn the circle over and glue two more beaks and one more tail triangle to the circle to match the beak and tail on the front. Add an eye to both sides of the circle with black marker.
3. Fold the rectangle into three equal sections. Tape the ends together, and cut a slit in the middle of one of the sides. This will be the little chick's feet. Slide the bottom of the circle into the slit, and your chick will stand on its own.

Cushy-Soft Easter Eggs

felt ● lace or ribbon ● cotton balls

1. For each egg, cut two ovals from felt. Glue lace or ribbon on the ovals for decoration.
2. Turn the ovals to the undecorated side. Spread glue on the edges of the ovals, and place a few cotton balls in the center of one oval.
3. Place the second oval on top of the first, pressing the ovals together at the edges.

"Cotton Bob" the Bunny

lightweight cardboard ●
cardboard tube ● cotton ●
construction paper

1. To make the body, cut legs and paws from lightweight cardboard, and glue them to a cardboard tube. Cover the body, legs, and paws with glue and cotton.
2. Cut ears, eyes, whiskers, nose, and mouth from construction paper. Glue them to the bunny body. Add a large cotton ball for the tail.

Easter Blossom Place Mat

white poster board ● colored tissue paper ● old newspaper ● paper towel ● clear self-adhesive paper

1. Cut a piece of white poster board to measure about 12 inches by 18 inches.
2. Cut colored tissue paper in the shapes of flower petals and leaves.

3. Cover your work surface with old newspaper.
4. Place a tissue petal on a paper towel and brush it with watered-down glue. Place the petal on the poster board. Continue until your design is finished.
5. Cut a piece of clear self-adhesive paper larger than the poster board. Ask an adult to help you remove the backing. Place the adhesive paper over your design. Fold the edges to the back and trim if necessary.

"Spring"-Time Bunny Card

construction paper ● cotton ball

1. Draw a bunny on white construction paper and cut it out.
2. Glue it to the inside of a piece of folded paper so that half is on one side of the fold and half is on the other. Add paper ears and a cotton-ball tail. Write a message inside.
3. Make the spring by cutting two strips of paper and folding as shown.

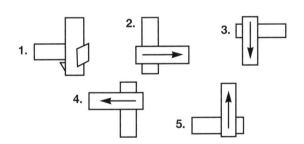

Glue the spring between the two halves of the card.
4. Write a greeting on the front of the card.

29

Jelly Bean Maze

construction paper ●
box lid ●
lightweight cardboard ●
clear tape ● jelly bean

1. Cut a piece of construction paper to fit the bottom of a box lid. Lightly pencil in your maze by creating L-shaped walls. Include one or two routes and several dead ends. Decorate the routes with markers. Then glue the maze in place.

2. Cut cardboard strips to match your pencil lines. Fold each strip where needed and tape to the maze floor. Use tape on both sides of the walls. Run your fingernail over the tape to make sure the tape holds.

3. Draw a rabbit and a basket onto cardboard and cut them out. Tape the rabbit at the maze's start and the basket at the finish.

4. To play, drop a jelly bean by the rabbit. See if you can get the jelly bean to the basket.

Three-Layer Card

construction paper ● plastic food wrap ● permanent markers

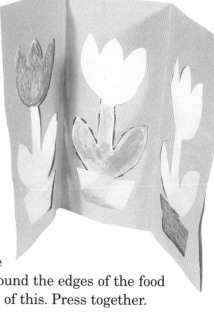

1. For each card, place two sheets of 9-by-12-inch construction paper on top of each other. On the 12-inch side of each sheet, draw a vertical line at 4 inches and at 8 inches, dividing the sheets into three panels.

2. Cut a tulip from the center of another piece of paper measuring 4 by 9 inches. Using this as a stencil, trace the design on each panel and cut out the tulips.

3. Spread glue around the edges of one sheet of paper and the tulip design. Place a piece of plastic food wrap on top. Spread glue around the edges of the food wrap. Place the other piece of paper on top of this. Press together.

4. Using a marker, color one section of the plastic-wrap tulip design on one panel only. Use another marker and color another section of the design on another panel. Then color the last panel with a third marker. Fold the outside panels over the center panel so the designs overlap.

Spring Bracelets

plastic-foam cup ● yarn ● felt

1. Draw a line about 1 inch from the top of a plastic-foam cup. Cut around the cup on the line, making the bracelet form.
2. Wrap yarn around the bracelet. Glue the ends to the inside. Glue on flowers cut from felt.

Pencil Pal

chenille stick ● felt ● pompoms ● construction paper ● twist ties

1. Make a spring with a chenille stick by wrapping it around a pencil six or seven times.
2. Cut ears and the inside ears out of pink and white felt and glue them together. Glue the ears onto a 1½-inch pompom.
3. Draw eyes on a piece of construction paper, and glue them in place.
4. Color the twist ties black. Glue them onto the pompom for whiskers. Apply glue to a ½-inch pompom, then press it on top of the twist-tie whiskers.
5. Glue the head to the top of the chenille stick.

Boxy Bunny

half-gallon milk carton ● construction paper ● cardboard tube ● plastic grass ● cotton ball

1. To make the basket, cut a half-gallon milk carton so that a 2-inch-high box is left. Cover with construction paper.
2. To make the head, cover a cardboard tube with construction paper. Decorate with cut-paper features for the bunny's face.
3. Cut out bunny ears. Glue the ears between the basket and the bunny's head. Hold together with paper clips until the glue is dry. Add plastic grass and a cotton-ball tail.

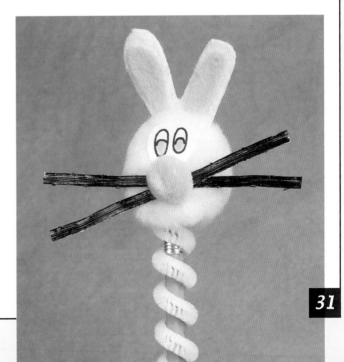

Ladybug Sun Catcher

clear plastic lid ● red tissue paper ●
felt ● wiggle eye ● chenille stick
● yarn

1. Cut a clear plastic lid in half.
   Poke three holes across the
   bottom for legs and one on top for hanging.
2. Mix a small batch of watered-down glue. Layer on
   small squares of red tissue paper. Dip your fingers in
   glue and smooth each piece with your fingers.
3. Glue on black felt spots, a black felt head, and a wiggle eye. Let dry.
4. Snip a black chenille stick into four pieces. Fold them in half. Poke three through the leg holes.
   For the antennae, snip a small hole in the head and carefully insert the fourth piece.
5. String yarn through the top hole, and hang your springtime ladybug in a sunny window.

Shell Chick

eggshell ● paint or egg dye ● string ●
peanut ● paper ● plastic grass

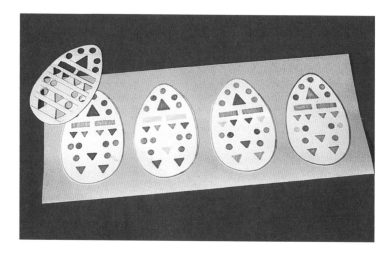

1. Wash and dry an eggshell half. Paint or
   dye the shell and let dry.
2. Glue a loop of string inside the shell
   for a hanger.
3. Paint an unshelled peanut.
4. When dry, glue on a paper beak. Use a
   marker to make eyes.
5. Glue some plastic grass in the egg. Glue
   the chick in the grass.

Egg-Stencil Card

construction paper ● heavy white paper ●
permanent markers

1. Fold a piece of construction paper in half to
   make a card.
2. Cut an egg shape from heavy white paper. Cut
   small shapes from the egg with a hole punch
   and scissors to make a stencil.
3. Place the egg stencil on white paper. Color around
   the egg and in the holes with permanent markers.
   Cut out the eggs and glue them to the outside of
   the card. Write a message inside.

Hoppin' Sock Bunny

construction paper ● two spring-type clothespins ● old sock
● two chenille sticks

1. From paper, cut out bunny ears long enough to cover spring-type clothespins. Glue the ears to the clothespins.
2. Cut out eyes and a nose from paper. Glue them to the bottom of an old sock. Insert two chenille sticks through the front of the sock to make whiskers.
3. Place your hand inside the sock, and clip the bunny ears to the heel of the sock.

Little Sheep

small wooden spools ●
plastic-foam egg ● plastic-foam ball ●
wiggle eyes ● chenille stick ● yarn

1. Paint four tiny wooden spools black and let dry.
2. Glue the spools onto the bottom of a plastic-foam egg. Glue on a plastic-foam ball for the head. Add wiggle eyes. Let dry.
3. Cut four small pieces of chenille stick, bend in half, and poke one on either side of the head for the sheep's ears, one for the tail, and one for the nose.
4. Tie a yarn bow around the sheep's neck.

Pumpkin-Seed Daisies

poster board ● chenille sticks ● pumpkin seeds ● clay ●
round food container ● fabric

1. For each flower, cut a 1-inch circle from poster board. With a pen, poke two small holes in the center of each circle.
2. Insert one end of a chenille stick through the holes and wrap it around the stem underneath the circle. Glue pumpkin seeds on the top of the circle to create flower petals.
3. Loop pieces of chenille sticks and twist them onto the stems for leaves.
4. Press clay into a round food container to hold the stems.
5. Cover the outside of the container with glue and fabric.

Eggshell Mosaic

eggshells ● paper or cardboard

1. Save the shells from hard-boiled, dyed eggs. Break the shells into small pieces.
2. Using a pencil, lightly draw a design on paper or cardboard. Glue the shell pieces onto it. Or glue them onto a design from a greeting card or a tissue box.
3. Hang up your mosaic, or give it as a gift.

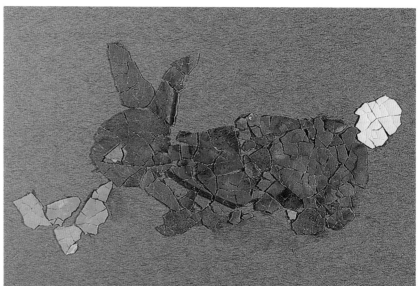

Spring Carryall

construction paper

1. With a ruler and a pencil, mark a 9-by-12-inch piece of construction paper as shown.
2. Cut on the solid lines. Cut little holes in the larger sections. Fold on all the dotted lines as shown.
3. Glue the bottom flaps in place and glue the basket together at the edges. Cut out a long narrow strip of paper, and glue it to the basket for the handle.
4. Decorate the sides with cutout paper.

2½″	3″	2½″	3″	1″
	2″			
Handle				

Mail-a-Chick

small white envelope ● paper

1. Open the flap of a small white envelope. With the back of the envelope facing you, draw the eyes and beak of a chick on the flap.
2. Draw wings on the side flaps.
3. Color your chick yellow and glue it to a piece of paper. Draw legs on the paper.
4. Write your greeting on a piece of paper, and tuck it in the envelope.

Peter Cottontail Decoration

craft sticks ● construction paper ● yarn

1. To make the fence, overlap and glue together the ends of seven craft sticks, as shown in the picture.
2. Draw a bunny on construction paper, and cut it out. Use markers to add a face.
3. Draw four eggs on construction paper, and cut them out. Decorate them by gluing on cut-paper stripes and punched-paper circles.
4. Glue one egg to the front of the bunny. Glue the other eggs and the bunny to the fence.
5. Tie a yarn hanger to the fence.

Jack Rabbit

2½-inch plastic-foam ball ● plastic-foam cup ● paper ● broom straw ● ribbon ● cotton ball

1. Glue a 2½-inch plastic-foam ball to the bottom of a plastic-foam cup.
2. Cut paper eyes, a nose, and a mouth, and glue them to the ball. Make slits in the top of the head with a table knife and insert paper ears. Push in pieces of broom straw for whiskers.
3. Tie a ribbon around the neck. Add circles of ribbon for buttons. Glue a ring of ribbon to the bottom of the cup. Add a cotton-ball tail.

Cardboard Tulips

cardboard egg carton ● chenille sticks ●
large frozen-juice container ● construction paper ● yarn

1. To make the flowers, cut out the cup sections from a cardboard egg carton. Trim the corners, making the shape of a tulip petal. Paint the cups and let dry.
2. Poke a hole in the bottom of each cup. Push a chenille stick through the hole for a stem. Tie a knot about 1 inch away from the other end for the stamen. Add glue and let dry.
3. Cover a large frozen-juice container with construction paper. Wrap yarn around the container and tie a bow. Cut long tulip leaves from paper, and place them in the container along with the tulips.

Bunny and Chick Box

aluminum-foil box ● construction paper ● poster board ● plastic grass

1. With scissors, cut the metal edge from the front of an aluminum-foil box. Cover the sides and the front of the box with construction paper. Tape to hold in place.
2. Trim off the top lid edge and cut seven tabs as shown.
3. Draw and cut out rabbits and chicks from poster board. Decorate with markers.

Glue them to the front of the tabs.
4. Fill the box with plastic grass.

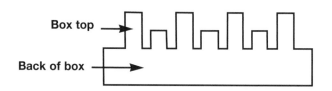

Box top →

Back of box →

Three Chicks

plastic-foam trays ● ribbon ● construction paper
● plastic grass

1. Cut chicks from plastic-foam trays. Add a ribbon bow around the neck of each chick and glue on paper-dot eyes.
2. Turn over a plastic-foam tray so the bottom is facing up. Make a slit where you want each chick to sit, using the point of a pencil.
3. Place each chick in a slit with some glue. Brush glue around the chicks on the tray. Press plastic grass into the glue and around the chicks. Let dry.

Woolly Sheep Card

construction paper ●
self-adhesive reinforcement rings

1. Fold a piece of construction paper in half to make a card. Draw a lamb on the front.
2. To make its wool look curly, cover the lamb's body with self-adhesive reinforcement rings.
3. Add grass, flowers, and other scenery. Write a message inside.

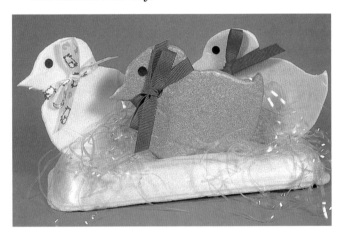

Scrambled Eggs

paper plate ● craft stick ● plastic soda bottle ● plastic grass ● cardboard ● plastic eggs

1. Paint a paper plate and a craft stick. Fill a soda bottle with plastic grass. Cut out two small circles of cardboard about the size of a silver dollar.
2. Push a craft stick through the center of the plate. Make slits in the centers of each of the cardboard circles. Slide a circle along each end of the craft stick. Glue the circles to the plate.
3. Play Scrambled Eggs by putting the plate on top of the bottle. Take turns placing the eggs on the plate. The player who topples the plate, or "scrambles the eggs," is out. Keep playing until you have a winner.

Blooming Lilies

construction paper ● chenille sticks ● clay ● plastic-foam cup ● tissue paper ● aluminum foil ● ribbon

1. For each lily, draw and cut a circle from construction paper. Cut a slit to the center of the circle. Glue the ends together, making a cone shape. Cut six small points around the edge of each lily. Curl the points back around a pencil.
2. Cut a tiny hole in the pointed end of each lily. Curl one end of a chenille stick, and push the other end through the hole, making the stamen and stem.
3. Draw and cut two identical paper stem-and-leaf sections for each lily. Make the stem wide enough for the chenille stick to fit onto. Place the chenille stick between the two leaf sections and glue together.
4. Place clay in the bottom of a plastic-foam cup. Press the stems of the lilies into the clay. Add some tissue paper on top. Wrap the cup with aluminum foil, and add a bow.

Dandy Dragonfly Mobile

craft sticks ● clear plastic container ● wiggle eyes ● string ● stick

1. For each dragonfly, paint or color two craft sticks.
2. Cut out two sets of wings from a clear plastic container. (See diagram.) Use a marker to decorate them.
3. Glue the wings between the craft sticks. Add wiggle eyes.
4. Use string to tie several dragonflies onto a stick and to make a hanger.

Easter-Egg Chain

heavy white paper ● ribbon

1. Cut out eggs from heavy white paper. The more eggs, the longer the chain will be.
2. In the middle of each egg, cut two vertical slits. Using markers, draw designs on the eggs.
3. Form the chain by weaving a long piece of ribbon through the slits in each egg.

Chicken Little Rising Card

poster board

1. Fold a long piece of poster board in half. Open the card, and draw an egg on the bottom half just below the fold. On the top half, just above the fold, draw a chick coming out of the egg.
2. Write a message on the egg, and color the drawing with crayons or markers. Cut around the outline of the chick with scissors just to the fold of the paper. Fold back the card so it will stand up.

Clothespin Bunny Magnet

clothespin ● thread ● tissue paper ● ribbon ● magnetic strip

1. Paint a clothespin white and let dry. Color the long sides of the clothespin with a pink marker to make the inside of each ear.
2. Draw eyes on your bunny with a black marker. Glue pieces of thread to the clothespin to make whiskers. Crunch a small piece of pink tissue paper into a ball, and glue it to the center of the whiskers for a nose. Use black marker to add a snout and pink marker to add a tiny tongue.
3. If you like, you can glue a small ribbon bow just below the ears. Glue a magnetic strip to the back of the bunny's head.

Cotton-Plate Bunny

two paper plates ● construction paper ● cotton ● chenille sticks ● yarn

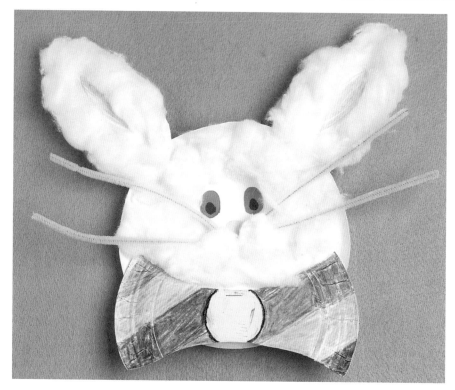

1. Use one paper plate for the rabbit's head. Cut another paper plate as shown to make the ears and a bow tie. Staple them to the head.

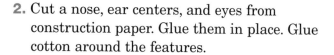

Bow tie　　**Ears**

2. Cut a nose, ear centers, and eyes from construction paper. Glue them in place. Glue cotton around the features.

3. Add whiskers made from chenille sticks. Color the bow tie.

4. Punch a hole at the top of the head, and tie on a yarn hanger.

Hopping Bunny

plastic milk carton ● round self-adhesive label

1. Cut a 1-by-5-inch strip from a white plastic milk carton.
2. Round the corners at one end of the strip. At the other end, cut 1-inch-long bunny ears and a 1-inch head.
3. Color a bunny face on a round self-adhesive label, then place it on the plastic strip.
4. Bend the bunny into a zigzag shape as shown. Press down and release the bunny to make it hop. How high can you make it hop? How far?
5. Make extra bunnies with different-colored faces. Challenge friends to see who can be the first to get all of his or her bunnies into an empty Easter basket.

Place-Card Flower

plastic spoon ● 1-inch plastic-foam ball ● poster board ● toothpicks

1. Paint the bowl part of a plastic spoon to look like a flower and let it dry. Paint the handle to look like a stem.
2. Press a 1-inch plastic-foam ball against a hard surface to flatten one side. Glue it to a piece of poster board. Push the stem of the flower into the ball.
3. Cut leaves from poster board, and glue each leaf onto a toothpick, leaving the pointed end of the toothpick showing on the bottom. Push the leaves into the ball.
4. Write a name on a piece of poster board. Glue it to a small piece of toothpick, and push it into the ball in front of the flower.

Cupcake Doll

blown egg ● cardboard tube ● paper baking cups ● permanent marker ● ribbon ● paper

1. Blow out an egg, following the directions on page 4, and set it aside.
2. Use a cardboard tube for the body. Cut out the bottoms from paper baking cups, and slip them over the tube for the dress. Add tape if needed.
3. Glue the egg to the top of the tube and let dry. Draw facial features with a permanent marker.
4. Tie a ribbon around the doll's neck. Fold a baking cup to look like a bonnet, and glue it to the head. Add cut-paper flowers.

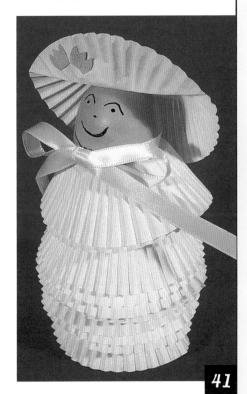

Easter Tree

container ● construction paper ● fallen tree branch ● sand ● plastic grass ● poster board ● ribbon

1. Decorate a container with construction paper.
2. Place a fallen tree branch in the container and pour sand around it. Place plastic grass on the sand.
3. From poster board, cut out shapes such as eggs, rabbits, birds, butterflies, and flowers. Use a marker to add details.
4. Punch a hole in each shape. Use ribbon to tie the shapes to the branches.

Fruity Easter Card

unsweetened fruit-drink powder ● water ● white nontoxic paint ● poster board ● foam paper

1. Mix unsweetened fruit-drink powder with a few drops of water.
2. Add white nontoxic paint and mix thoroughly.
3. Fold a piece of poster board in half to make a card and paint on "fruity" Easter greetings. Let dry.
4. Glue on oranges made from foam paper.
5. Send this to a friend for Easter. He or she can scratch the greeting and sniff the fruity aroma.

Woolly Sheep

cereal box ● wiggle eyes ● cotton balls ● yarn

1. Cut off the back of a cereal box and fold it in half so that the label faces inward. Cut out the shape of a sheep using the folded edge as the sheep's back.
2. Color the sheep's legs and head with a black marker. Glue on two wiggle eyes.
3. Spread glue on the sheep's body. Stretch out cotton balls and press them firmly into the glue.
4. Tie a yarn bow around the sheep's neck to help it stand.

Candy Cone

ice-cream cone ● plastic food wrap ● ribbon

1. Fill an empty ice-cream cone with assorted candies.
2. Cut a circle from plastic food wrap, and lay it over the top of the cone. Tie two ribbons around the top rim of the cone, and knot at opposite sides.
3. Bring the four ends of the ribbons up, and tie them together in a bow to make a handle. Hang the cone basket on someone's doorknob.

Foam-Flower Picture

construction paper ● poster board ●
plastic-foam egg cartons

1. For the background of your picture, glue a piece of blue construction paper to a piece of poster board.
2. Cut out stems and leaves from green paper, and glue to the background.
3. Cut out plastic-foam egg carton cups. Trim the cups to look like flowers. Glue them to the stems.
4. Add a paper butterfly in the sky.

Nesting Chick

cardboard egg carton ● yarn ● eggshell ●
construction paper

1. Cut a cup section from a cardboard egg carton. Spread glue around the outside of the cup. Press the end of a piece of yarn into the glue, and wind the yarn around the cup.
2. Glue pieces of yarn of a different color inside the nest for straw.
3. Paint half of an eggshell. Add features cut from paper, and glue the chick inside the nest.

Tape the Tail

foam paper ● cotton balls

1. Make a bunny out of foam paper.
2. Put circles of tape on cotton balls.
3. Hang the bunny on the wall. Grab some friends and take turns trying to "Tape the Tail" on the bunny while blindfolded.

Puffy Snail

old tube sock ● paper towels ● chenille stick
● wiggle eyes

1. Stuff an old sock with paper towels. Roll the sock, starting with the open end, until it is almost rolled completely to create a shell. Glue in place and let dry.
2. Paint the shell and let dry.
3. Poke a chenille stick through the head to make antennae. Twist the ends into small circles and glue a wiggle eye onto each one.
4. Glue on a piece of yarn to make a smile. Glue on a swirl of yarn to complete the shell.

Shiny Metallic Card

heavy white paper ● shiny gift wrap

1. Fold a piece of heavy white paper in half to make a card.
2. Cut a scalloped edge at the bottom of the front of the card. Glue a strip of shiny gift wrap on the inside bottom of the back half of the card.
3. Cut flowers from the same shiny gift wrap, and glue them to the front of the card. Add stems and leaves with marker.

Button Blossoms

chenille sticks ●
large, flat two-hole buttons ●
poster board ● lightweight fabric

1. Insert a chenille stick through one hole in a large, flat button and back through the other hole. Twist the ends together under the button to make a stem.
2. Spread glue on a piece of poster board and press a piece of lightweight fabric on top. Let dry.
3. Cut out several fabric petals, and glue them to the underside of the button.
4. Bend short pieces of chenille stick into leaf shapes, and twist them onto the stem.

Bunny-Weave Basket

colored paper or ribbon ● plastic berry basket ●
cotton ball ● buttons ● chenille stick ● plastic grass

1. Cut strips of colored paper or ribbon.
2. Weave the paper or ribbon through the "bars"
   of a plastic berry basket. Tape or glue the ends
   in place.
3. To make the tail, glue a cotton ball to one side
   of the basket. Tape or glue paper ears inside
   the basket on the opposite side.
4. Glue on button eyes and a nose. Add a mouth
   cut from paper.
5. To make a handle, attach a chenille stick from
   one side of the basket to the other. Fill the
   basket with plastic grass.

Rabbit-Ears Puppet

cardboard egg carton ● construction paper ● toothpicks ●
poster board ● ribbon

1. Cut one cup section from
   a cardboard egg carton.
   Paint it and let dry.
2. To make the head, cut eyes,
   a nose, and a mouth from
   construction paper. Glue
   them to the bottom of the cup.
3. Paint six toothpicks for
   whiskers. Poke three
   holes on each side of
   the cup. Place the
   whiskers in the holes
   with glue.
4. Cut a small strip of poster
   board, and glue it to the
   back of the rabbit's head.
   Leave enough room so two
   fingers will fit inside. Glue
   a bow under his chin.

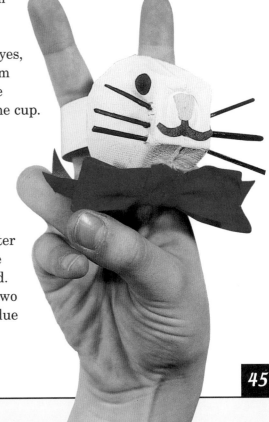

45

Sports Bunny

salt container ● felt ● plastic dessert cup ● cardboard

1. Cover the top third of a salt container with white felt, the second third with a different color, and the bottom third with another color.
2. Cover a plastic dessert cup with felt. Cut a brim from cardboard and cover with felt. Glue it to the hat, and glue the hat to the head.
3. Trace the bottom of the can onto cardboard. Draw two feet extending from the circle. Cut out the shape as one piece. Trace the shape onto felt and cut it out. Glue the cardboard and felt feet together, then glue the feet to the bottom of the can.
4. Cut two arms from cardboard and cover both sides with felt. Glue on sleeves. Glue the arms in place. Cut two ears from cardboard. Cover both sides with felt, and glue in place.
5. From felt, cut out and glue on two eyes, a mouth, and nose. Decorate your Sports Bunny as you like.

Easter Bookmark

plastic-foam tray ● gift wrap ● yarn

1. Draw a cross on a plastic-foam tray. Cut it out.
2. Trace the cross twice onto gift wrap. Cut them out and glue them to each side of the plastic-foam cross.
3. Use a hole punch to make a hole in the bottom of the cross.
4. Braid together three 20-inch lengths of yarn. Knot together the top and bottom of the braid to form a loop.
5. Push the center of the braid loop through the hole in the cross. Then bring the knotted ends up through the loop and pull them snugly.

Filter Flowers

coffee filters ● water ●
food coloring ● waxed paper ●
chenille sticks

1. For each flower, fold a coffee filter into quarters. Dampen the filter with water. Add drops of food coloring onto the filter.
2. Press the filter between pieces of waxed paper to spread the color. Open the filter, and let it dry on paper towels.
3. Fold the filter in quarters again, forming a point at the bottom. Twist a chenille stick around the point for a stem.

Rabbit Basket

construction paper ● yarn

1. Fold a piece of construction paper in half. Cut out a basket, using the fold as the bottom. Glue the sides together.
2. Cut a paper handle and glue the ends inside the basket. Decorate the front.
3. Make a bunny from two circles of paper. Add ears, eyes, and a nose from paper. Glue on yarn whiskers. Write an Easter message on the bunny's body, and slip the bunny inside the basket.
4. Cut a small gift tag from paper. On it write the name of the person the card is for and "Please pull out the bunny." Attach it to the handle of the basket with a piece of yarn.

Chicken-and-the-Egg Card

poster board ● construction paper ● gift wrap

1. Draw three egg shapes, touching each other, on white poster board. Cut around them to make the shape shown.
2. Color one side of the eggs yellow. Make a bill and eyes for the chick from construction paper, and glue them to the center egg.
3. Fold the outer eggs over the center one. Draw a zigzag line down the center of the egg on top, and cut along the line. Fold over the cut egg, trace along the zigzag edge on the white egg underneath, and then cut along the edge. Unfold the eggs.
4. Glue gift wrap to the outside of each egg half and let dry. Trim around the edges with scissors. Write a message inside the card.

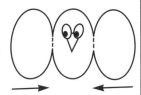

Fold on dotted line.

Rabbit Jewelry Set

pompoms ● chenille sticks ● felt ● wiggle eyes

1. For the bracelet, glue a ¼-inch pompom to each end of a chenille stick. Set aside to dry.
2. Glue on two ½-inch pink pompoms for cheeks, a ¼-inch black pompom for a nose, a pink felt tongue, and small wiggle eyes on a 1½-inch white pompom.
3. Cut a white chenille stick in half. Fold each piece in half and twist the ends together.

Glue these into the head for ears. Glue the rabbit head to the center of the chenille stick.
4. Make the ring the same way you made the bracelet, using smaller pieces.
5. To wear the jewelry, wrap the chenille sticks around your wrist and finger and twist the ends together.

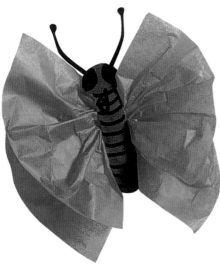

Butterfly Clip

tissue paper ● jumbo paper clip ● construction paper

1. To make wings, cut two 4-inch-by-4-inch squares of tissue paper.
2. Slide one square onto a jumbo paper clip, squishing it as you go. Repeat with the second square.
3. Cut out and decorate construction paper to look like the head, feelers, and body. Glue it on top of the paper clip.
4. Glue the butterfly to a homemade greeting card, or use it to make a three-dimensional picture.

Miniature Easter Basket

plastic ring and cap from soda bottle ● cardboard ● plastic grass or shredded paper ● navy beans

1. Fit the plastic ring from a soda-bottle cap into the cap to form a basket handle. Cut a small circle of cardboard to fit inside the cap.
2. Ask an adult to help you apply glue from a hot-glue gun into the bottom of the cap. Press the cardboard into the cap, sandwiching the bottom of the ring between the cardboard and the cap.
3. Glue plastic grass or shredded paper to the cardboard.
4. Use markers to color navy beans, and then glue them onto the grass.

Loop Bunny

construction paper ● yarn

1. Cut pink paper into strips that are 1 inch wide. Make one long strip for the body, three shorter strips for the head and ears, and four even shorter strips for the four legs.
2. Roll the body and head strips into circle shapes, and tape the ends together. Tape the head circle to the body circle. Hold the ends of each ear strip together to make a raindrop shape, and tape the ends together. Tape the ears to the head.
3. Roll the four remaining strips into circles and tape the ends together. Tape these to the body of the rabbit for legs.
4. Attach yarn to the head of the rabbit between the ears for a hanger.

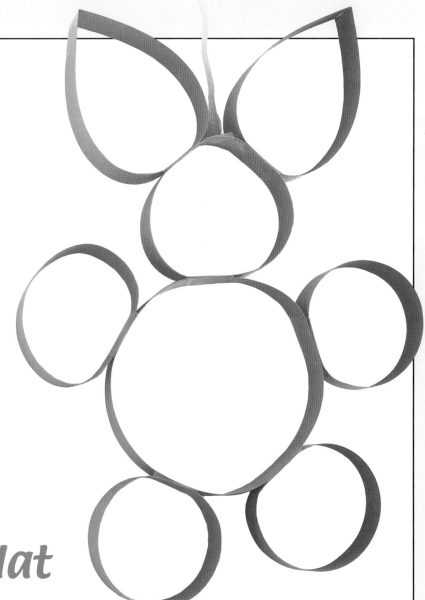

Easter-Egg Mat

construction paper

1. Place a sheet of construction paper 12 inches by 18 inches lengthwise in front of you. Cut vertical slits 8 inches long and 2 inches apart.
2. Using paper of another color, cut three strips 2 inches by 18 inches. Weave them in and out of the slits on the large sheet of paper to form a checkerboard pattern. Glue down the ends of the strips.
3. Add colorful paper eggs to the squares.

Hanging Bouquet

construction paper ● ribbon ● cardboard
● silk or dried flowers

1. Fold a square piece of construction paper as shown in A. At the top point, draw a circle the size of a doorknob and cut it out as shown in B.
2. Fold up the bottom point of the paper to meet the top edge as shown in C, and staple to hold the shape. Glue a ribbon bow on top of the staple.
3. To reinforce the hole, cut a hole in a square piece of cardboard to match the size of the hole in the paper. Glue the cardboard hole to the back of the paper behind the hole.
4. Fill the basket with silk or dried flowers and hang it on a doorknob as a gift.

Fluffy White Rabbit

cardboard ● felt ● cotton balls ● buttons ●
black yarn ● string

1. Draw and cut out a rabbit shape from cardboard. Cover the ears with pieces of pink felt. Outline them with glue and cotton balls.
2. Spread glue over the rest of the rabbit, and completely cover it with cotton balls.
3. From felt, cut out and glue on eyes, a nose, and a bow tie. Glue buttons onto the body. Glue on black yarn for the mouth.
4. Attach a piece of short string to the top of the rabbit for a hanger.

Stained-Glass Picture

paper ● waxed paper ● black fabric paint ● food coloring ● craft sticks

1. Draw a small picture on paper, no bigger than 3½ inches high and 3½ inches wide. Place waxed paper over the drawing and trace your picture with fabric paint. Let dry overnight.
2. Mix food coloring with glue, and color your picture. Color or paint four craft sticks. Let dry.
3. Glue the craft sticks together to make a square frame and let dry. Glue the frame to the waxed paper and trim off the excess. If you'd like, attach string to the picture and hang it in a window.

Lilies on the Pond

plastic-foam egg carton ● glass bowl ● water ● blue food coloring

1. For each flower, scallop the edges of two cups cut from a plastic-foam egg carton. Glue one inside the other.
2. Cut leaves from the flat part of the carton. Glue the flower on top.
3. In the kitchen sink, fill a bowl with water colored with blue food coloring. Float the lilies on the water.
4. Have an adult help you place the bowl in the center of the dining-room table.

Chick Rocker

small paper plate ● construction paper

1. Fold a small paper plate in half.
2. Draw and cut out two chicks the same size from construction paper. Glue the chicks together from their heads to the middle of their bodies.
3. Place the chicks on the fold of the paper plate so that half the chick is on each side. Glue in place.
4. Add features with markers. Stand the chick rocker on a table and make it rock.

Pinecone Hyacinth

pinecone ● plastic cap
● colored aluminum foil ●
tissue paper ● ribbon
● construction paper

1. Glue a pinecone upright in a plastic cap covered with colored aluminum foil.
2. Cut tissue paper into 1½-inch squares. Put the point of a pencil in the center of the tissue. Gently twist the paper around the pencil point. Dip the tip into glue, and stick it between the petals of the pinecone.
3. Add a bow. Make leaves out of green paper and glue them in place.

Tube O' Tulips

cardboard tube ●
construction paper ● cardboard
● chenille sticks

1. Spread glue on a cardboard tube, and cover it with paper. Cut a circle from a piece of cardboard for the base, and glue paper on top of it.
2. Glue the tube to the base. Glue on a paper flower.
3. Cut two flower shapes from paper for each flower. Place a chenille stick in between them and glue together.
4. Place the flowers in the tube.

Bunny Note Holder

spring-type clothespin ● construction paper
● wiggle eyes ● pompoms ●
small magnetic strip

1. Paint a spring-type clothespin white.
2. Draw and cut out a bunny's head from pink construction paper. Add white trim for the ears and a bow tie. Glue on wiggle eyes and a pompom nose and cheeks. Glue the head to the clothespin with the closed part facing down. Let dry.
3. Glue a magnetic strip to the back. Let dry.

Woody Long-Ears Card

construction paper ● two large craft sticks ● foam paper ● gift wrap

1. Fold a 10-by-12-inch piece of construction paper in half.
2. Paint two large craft sticks with white poster paint. They will need two coats of paint to cover completely.
3. Glue the craft sticks on the front of the card for the bunny's ears. Cut a circle from white foam paper for the bunny's head. Add pink construction paper to the ears.
4. Cut a tie from gift wrap, and glue it in place. Make a face with markers and foam paper. Write a message inside.

Bunny-Basket Place Card

plastic dessert cup ● raffia ● poster board ● plastic grass ● jelly beans

1. Punch twelve holes below the rim of a plastic dessert cup.
2. Lace raffia through the holes.
3. Braid strips of raffia to make a handle. Slip the ends of the handle through a hole on each side of the basket and tie knots in the ends. Tie a ribbon to the handle.
4. Draw a bunny on poster board. Write a name on it. Cut it out and place it in the basket on top of plastic grass.
5. Add jelly beans or other bite-sized treats. Place a bunny basket in front of each person's place setting.

Basket of Flowers

half-gallon milk carton ● construction paper ●
white poster board ● spring-type clothespins ● margarine tub

1. Measure 3½ inches from the bottom of a half-gallon milk carton. Cut off the top and cover the bottom with construction paper to make a flowerpot.
2. From white poster board, cut two 5-by-11-inch pieces. Cut out a handle about ¾ inch from the top of each piece.
3. Glue paper the same color as the bottom half of the carton to the bottom of the white poster-board pieces. Cut and glue on a paper flower.
4. Glue the poster-board pieces on opposite sides of the carton, joining the handle at the top. Hold in place with spring-type clothespins until dry. Place a small flower plant in a margarine tub and put it inside the basket.

Napkin Chick

poster board ● paper napkin

1. Draw and cut a chick from a piece of poster board. Add an eye and a beak using poster paint.
2. Draw and cut out a circle from the middle of the chick.
3. Insert a paper napkin through the hole. Place one chick with a napkin for each guest at the dinner table.

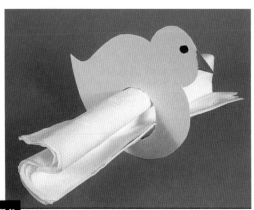

Hatching Chick Card

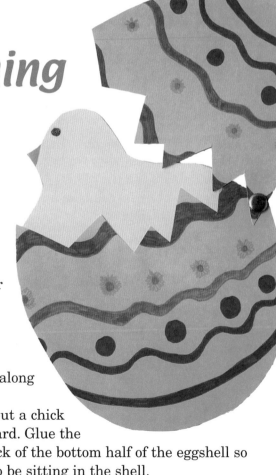

poster board ●
metal fastener

1. Draw and cut out an egg shape on poster board. Draw designs on the egg with markers. Cut the egg in half along a jagged line.
2. Draw and cut out a chick from poster board. Glue the chick to the back of the bottom half of the eggshell so that it seems to be sitting in the shell.
3. Attach the top half of the egg to the bottom half with a metal fastener. The egg can then be opened and closed.

Beaded Bookmark

thin wire ● beads ● narrow ribbon ● poster board

1. Bend thin wire in half. Use it as a threader by pushing it through the hole of one bead and threading ribbon through. Pull the wire along with the ribbon through the bead. Repeat with other beads.
2. Position the beads near each end of the ribbon. Make knots to hold the beads in place.
3. From poster board, cut three circles about 1 inch wide. Draw a caterpillar on one circle and a butterfly on another. Glue the circles together, sandwiching the ribbon and third blank circle in the middle.
4. Place a heavy book on top of the circle medallion. Allow it to dry thoroughly. Cover the medallion with plastic food wrap if the glue oozes a bit.

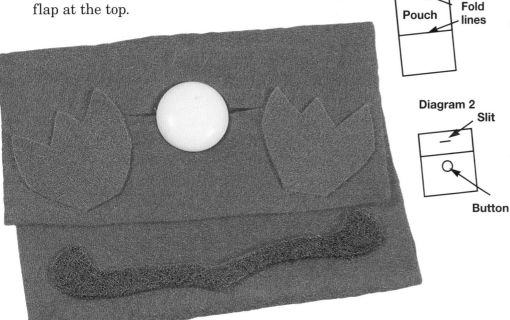

Easter Purse

felt ● needle ● thread ● button

1. Cut a strip of felt 9 inches by 4½ inches. Fold the felt strip as shown in Diagram 1, leaving a 2-inch flap at the top.

Diagram 1

Flap

Pouch

Fold lines

Diagram 2

Slit

Button

2. Glue along the sides to form a pouch. Place a paper towel on top and then a heavy book to hold the pouch in place until the glue dries.
3. Sew a button to the pouch and cut a small slit in the flap as shown in Diagram 2. Button the pouch closed. Decorate with pieces of cut felt.

Bunny Puppet

heavy paper ● cardboard tube ● cotton ball

1. Cut a bunny shape from heavy paper. (Use a picture from a coloring book as a pattern, if you'd like.)
2. Draw or paint on bunny features.
3. Cut off 1 inch from a cardboard tube. Tape or staple the 1-inch-wide tube section to the back of the bunny. Glue a cotton ball to the bunny's tummy.
4. Put two or three of your fingers up through the tube section at the back of the bunny to play with your finger puppet.

Egg Shaker

beans, rice, or lentils ● plastic egg ● stickers

1. Place beans, rice, or lentils inside a plastic egg.
2. Glue the egg shut.
3. Decorate your egg with stickers.
4. Shake to play.

Quilted Flowerpot

fabric ● flowerpot

1. Cut scraps of fabric into 1-inch pieces.
2. Spread glue on a small area of the flowerpot and press the pieces of fabric into the glue. Continue until the entire flowerpot is covered.
3. When the fabric is dry, place a flower into the flowerpot.

Sunflower Lollipop

lollipop in cellophane ● construction paper ● paper clips

1. Use a medium-sized lollipop wrapped in cellophane for each flower.
2. Cut a strip of green construction paper ½ inch by 5 inches long for the stem. Glue one end of the strip at the bottom of the candy, and wind it around the stick. Glue it at the end. Add paper leaves. Hold the paper in place with paper clips if needed.
3. Cut out a 2-inch-round circle. Cut a small circle from the center. Trim around the edges to form a flower. Glue it on top of the candy. Round off the corners of the cellophane with scissors.

Box Basket

facial-tissue box ●
heavy white paper ● foam paper
paper clips ● plastic grass

1. Use a 3-by-9-by-5-inch facial-tissue box for the base of the basket. Trim around the opening so there is a 1-inch border.
2. Cut slits around the border. Paint them to look like straw. Paint the rest of the box another color.
3. Cut two identical eggs from 8-by-10-inch pieces of heavy white paper. Cut a handle at the top of the eggs. Decorate with foam-paper shapes. Glue the tops of the handles together.
4. Glue one egg to each side of the box. Hold in place with paper clips. Place plastic grass inside.

Tubular Chick Puppet

cardboard tube ●
construction paper

1. Cut points at one end of a cardboard tube. Paint the outside of the tube and let dry.
2. Cut a diamond-shaped beak, eyes, and feathers from construction paper. Glue them to the tube.
3. Place a couple of fingers in the bottom of the tube to work the chick puppet.

Find-the-Jelly-Bean Game

cardboard egg carton ● thread ● tissue paper ● heavy white paper ● cotton ● jelly bean

1. Cut three cups from a cardboard egg carton. To make each rabbit, turn the cups upside down, and use marker to draw eyes. Glue pieces of thread for whiskers. Crumple a small piece of tissue paper into a ball for the nose and glue it to the center of the whiskers. Add a snout with marker.
2. Draw and cut small ears from paper. Glue the ears to the back of the egg-carton section. Glue a small piece of cotton to the back below the ears for a fluffy tail.
3. To play the game, line up the rabbits on a tabletop and place a jelly bean under one of the rabbit cups. Slide the rabbit cups around to change their position in line, and challenge a friend or family member to pick the rabbit that is hiding the jelly bean.

Pompom Rabbit

pompoms ● wiggle eyes ● felt ● ribbon

1. Glue a 1-inch pompom to one side of a 2-inch pompom for a tail. Glue four 1-inch pompoms to the front for paws.
2. Glue a 1½-inch pompom on top of the body for the head. Glue pink pompoms on for cheeks. Glue a ¼-inch black pompom on for a nose. Glue on two wiggle eyes and a pink felt tongue.
3. Cut out two ears from white felt. Cut out two inner ears from pink felt. Glue them to the white ears. Separate the fur on the head, and glue the ears into the head. Add a ribbon bow.

Fork-Loom Corsage

thick yarn ● four-pronged fork ● cardboard ● construction paper ● safety pin

1. For each flower, weave a piece of thick yarn, about 2 feet long, through a four-pronged fork. Start at the base of the prongs, and weave in a figure-8 pattern by placing the yarn in front of the first two prongs. Then slip the yarn between the second and third prongs; wrap it behind the third and fourth prongs, then in front of them, back between the second and third prongs, behind the first and second prongs, in front of them, and so on. Continue until the fork is full of yarn.

2. Insert an 8-inch piece of green yarn below the wrapped yarn between the second and third prongs. Wrap the green yarn one time around all the yarn on the fork, and tie it loosely.

3. Slip all the yarn off the fork, and tighten the knot. Trim the excess yarn with scissors. Make flowers in a variety of colors, and glue them to a small piece of cardboard.

4. Glue leaves made from construction paper around the flowers. Glue a safety pin to the back of the corsage.

Curlique Lamb

cardboard tube ● black and white paper

1. Cut a cardboard tube about 2½ inches long. Roll a 4-inch-wide piece of black paper and insert it into one end of the tube with about 1½ inches sticking out.

2. Crease the paper and cut out the shape of a lamb's head. Glue the sides together. Cut a slit and glue on paper ears. Add eyes.

3. Roll four ½-inch-wide pieces of black paper tightly for the legs. Poke four holes in the tube and insert the legs. Add glue.

4. Cut a piece of white paper the same length as the lamb's body. Make it long enough to go over the body and hang down. Cut two more sheets of paper, each one a little shorter than the last. Cut slits at the ends, as shown.

Slit   Ears

Slits

5. Roll each slit over a pencil. Glue the curled paper so the curls are turned under. Glue on the longest sheet first and the shortest sheet last.

Secret Egg Card

construction paper ● plastic grass

1. Cut a 6-by-9-inch piece of construction paper. Fold it in half. On the front write, "Look for the hidden Easter message inside."
2. Draw eggs on white paper. Draw one with a 1-inch tab at the bottom.
3. Cut out the eggs. Color them with markers. Write your message on the back of the egg that has the tab.
4. On the inside of the card, spread glue and press plastic grass for a nest. Glue the eggs in place, but leave an unglued space in which to slip the tabbed egg.
5. The receiver of the card will need to hunt for the message.

"Egg"-cellent Flowers

small clay pot ● small plastic-foam ball ●
plastic eggs with holes at the top ● chenille sticks ● pompoms

1. Decorate a small clay pot. Let dry. Stuff the pot with a plastic-foam ball and trim any excess.
2. Paint the foam ball brown and let dry.
3. Open the eggs. Insert chenille sticks through the holes in the eggs and bend the ends to hold them in place. Glue pompoms inside each egg. Let dry.
4. Poke each flower stem into the plastic foam.

Easter Candle

small paper plate ● glitter ● cardboard tube
● construction paper

1. Spread glue around the rim of a small paper plate. Sprinkle glitter on the glue. Let dry and shake off the loose glitter.
2. Cover a cardboard tube with paper. Dip one end of the tube in glue, and place it in the center of the paper plate. Let dry. Add a paper flame.
3. Cut paper leaves and flower petals. Glue them around the candle. Wad up a piece of paper, and glue it in the center of the flower.

Easter Wreath

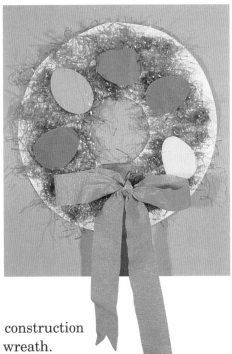

poster board ● yarn ● plastic grass ● construction paper ● crepe paper

1. Cut out a wreath shape from poster board. Tape a yarn hanger on the back.
2. Twist small clumps of plastic grass and glue them on the front.
3. Cut out egg shapes from construction paper. Glue them on the wreath.
4. Tie on a crepe-paper bow.

Fabric Flowers

fabric ● chenille sticks

1. Cut a piece of fabric 2½ inches wide and 8 inches long. Starting at the narrow end, fold over ⅓ inch and continue to fold into accordion pleats until the entire piece is pleated.
2. Bend one end of a long chenille stick around the center of the folded fabric, and twist it to make the stem. Pull the folded flower open into a circle.
3. For the leaves, loop and twist pieces of chenille stick onto the stem. Make several flowers, and place them in a vase.

Egg-Carton Bunny Basket

two plastic-foam egg cartons of the same color ● cotton balls ● construction paper ● fabric ●
one cardboard egg carton

1. Cut off the tops of both plastic-foam cartons and cut one of the bottoms in half the long way, making a row of six cups. Glue this row, upside down, over half of the other foam carton, leaving the other half for the basket.
2. Decorate the row of egg shapes with cotton noses and paper whiskers, eyes, ears, and heart shapes for feet. Glue them in place.
3. On every other bunny, glue on a bow of fabric to the top of the head.
4. Cut little hats from the cardboard carton's peaked dividers. Paint them black, and glue each to a circle of black paper. Glue the hats to the remaining bunny heads.

Bunny Candy Cup

cardboard egg carton ● thread ● tissue paper ● cotton ● plastic grass

1. From a cardboard egg carton, cut a section that contains one cup and two long pieces shaped like rabbit ears.
2. Color the insides of the ears with pink marker or paint. Draw eyes on the front of the cup with marker. Glue on thread pieces to make whiskers. Crumple a small piece of tissue paper into a ball, and glue it to the center of the whiskers. Use marker to draw a snout and tongue. Glue a small piece of cotton to the back of the cup for the tail.
3. Glue a small amount of plastic grass to the inside of the cup. Make several of these bunny cups, fill them with candy, and add them to your holiday table.

Chick-in-the-Grass Card

construction paper

1. Fold a piece of construction paper in the shape of a card. Write a message inside.
2. Cut a piece of paper to fit the width of the card, and make slits to look like grass. Glue it to the card.
3. Draw and cut out a chick. Glue it standing in the grass.

Puffy Chicken

paper ● felt ● needle ● thread ● cotton balls or scrap fabric

1. Draw the outline of a chicken about 10 inches tall on paper. Place the pattern on a piece of felt and draw around it with a pencil. Do this again and cut out both chickens.
2. Place the two chickens together with the pencil lines on the inside. Sew them together around the edge, leaving a small section open.
3. Stuff cotton balls or pieces of scrap fabric inside the chicken through the small opening. Finish sewing, stuffing as you go.
4. Glue felt eyes and wings to the chicken.

Yarn-Art Planter

plastic food container ● yarn

1. Spread an inch of glue around the outside bottom of a plastic food container.
2. Working from the bottom, press the end of a piece of yarn into the glue, and start winding it around the container. Use different colors of yarn. Glue a decoration on the front and let it dry.
3. Place small stones in the bottom of the container for drainage. Add some dirt and clippings from a growing plant, or place a potted plant in the container.

Index